5 More Steps to Mastering

Your Money

(Step 6 to 10)

Contents

Step 6: Build an emergency fund.

An emergency fund is good to have in place and forms a critical part of a financial plan. It is a pool of money reserved for unexpected expenses or income disruptions, such as job loss or medical emergencies. Building an emergency fund is crucial to avoiding debt in unforeseen circumstances.

To start building your emergency fund, set a realistic savings goal. A good emergency saving plan is to save at least four to six months of living expenses. This amount should cover your essential expenses, such as rent/mortgage, utilities, groceries, and transportation.

To reach your goal, start by creating a budget and identifying areas where you can cut back on expenses. Then, consider using automatic savings tools, such as direct deposit or automatic transfers, to make saving easier. You can also sell items you no longer need or take on a side hustle to boost your savings.

It's important to keep your emergency fund in a separate account that is easily accessible. For example, consider a high-yield savings account or a money market account offering better interest rates than a traditional one.

Remember, building an emergency fund takes time and patience, but the peace of mind it provides is priceless. Start small and stay consistent, and you'll be prepared for whatever life throws your way.

If you're finding it hard to build an emergency fund, consider starting with a small amount. Even $200 can provide some relief if an unexpected expense pops up. Once you've built that fund up to a reasonable amount, such as $900 or more (depending on your personal situation), start adding to it regularly and consistently. You'll be surprised at how quickly it adds up!

How to build an emergency fund?

Find out how much you need. You can do this by calculating your monthly expenses and multiplying them by three. This will give you the total amount of money you need to be able to cover any unexpected expenses that may come up. Next, start saving. Set aside a small amount each month to reach your goal quickly.

In life, unexpected situations can arise that require us to have financial reserves available to address them. These situations can range from unexpected medical expenses, job loss, and car repairs to natural disasters and other unexpected emergencies. Therefore, it is important to build an emergency fund to avoid financial stress and anxiety during these times. An emergency fund can be a pool of money that is set aside specifically for unforeseen circumstances.

How do you define Emergency saving?

An emergency fund can be a financial cushion that you can rely on during a financial crisis. It is a savings account that you set up specifically to handle unexpected expenses. These expenses can include anything from a sudden illness or injury to a significant home repair or car breakdown. Emergency funds are designed to be used when needed most, without relying on credit cards or loans.

Why is an Emergency Fund Important?

Having an emergency fund is essential for several reasons. First, it provides a sense of financial security. Knowing that you have a cushion of savings to fall back on can help alleviate the stress and anxiety that come with unexpected financial situations. Second, an emergency fund can help you avoid going into debt. When unexpected expenses arise, many people resort to using credit cards or taking out loans, leading to high-interest rates and debt. An emergency fund can help you avoid these situations and keep you financially stable.

How do you determine the amount you should Save in an Emergency Fund?

The amount you should save in an emergency fund varies depending on your individual circumstances. Financial experts recommend saving four to six months of living expenses in an emergency fund. This amount should cover your basic living expenses, such as housing, food, utilities, and transportation, in case of job loss or other unexpected events. However, you may need to save more if you have dependents or a higher risk of unexpected expenses.

How to Build an Emergency Fund

Building an emergency fund requires discipline and commitment. These are some steps you can take to build your emergency fund:

1. Determine Your Monthly Expenses

You first determine your monthly expenses. First, list all your monthly expenses, including rent/mortgage, utilities, food, transportation, and any other bills you have. This will give you a clear insight into how much money you need to put away each month to cover your basic living expenses.

1. Set a Savings Goal

Once you have determined your monthly expenses, set a savings goal for your emergency fund. Remember, you may need to save more if you have dependents or a higher risk of unexpected expenses. Set a realistic savings goal that you can achieve within a reasonable timeframe.

1. Create a Budget

A budget will help you track income and expenses and identify areas where you can reduce spending. Start by listing all sources of income. Next, list all your monthly expenses. Finally, compare your income to your expenses and identify areas where you can cut back. This could include eating out less, reducing your entertainment expenses, or cancelling subscriptions you don't need. By creating a budget, you can free up more money to put toward your emergency fund.

1. You should set up Automatic Pre Authorised-Savings.

This is the easiest way to build an emergency fund. First, set up an automatic monthly transfer from your checking account to your emergency fund. This way, you won't have to remember to transfer money manually and will be less likely to spend the money on non-essential expenses.

Step 7: Pay off high-interest debt.

If you're tired of constantly struggling to keep up with your high-interest debt payments, it's time to take control of your finances and pay off that high-interest debt.
The first step is to create a budget and stick to it. Then, analyze your monthly expenses and see where you can cut back. For example, can you eat out less often? Can you cancel that subscription service you rarely use? Every penny counts when it comes to paying off debt.
Next, consider consolidating your debt. If you have numerous credit cards or loans with high-interest rates, you may be able to save money over time by consolidating.

Another option is to negotiate with your creditors. Many credit card companies will work with you to lower your interest rate or create a payment plan that works for you.
Finally, consider a balance transfer. Some credit card companies offer promotional periods with 0% interest on balance transfers. This can be a great way to pay off your debt without accruing extra interest.
Remember, paying off high-interest debt takes time and effort, but it is ultimately worth it in the end. So take control of your finances and start living debt-free today.

Should you pay off high-interest debt before investing?
This is a common question among people trying to manage their finances effectively.
Unfortunately, the answer is complex, depending on your financial situation and goals.
In general, it is recommended to pay off high-interest debt before investing. This is because the interest rates on debt are usually higher than the potential returns on investments. For example, suppose you have credit card debt with an interest rate of 20%. In that case, it is unlikely that you will find an investment that will yield a higher return than 20%.

Additionally, paying off high-interest debt can help improve your credit score. A high enough credit score can make it simpler for you to be approved for loans and credit cards with reduced interest rates, thus saving you money. There are a few exceptions, though. For example, suppose you have low-interest debt (such as a mortgage or student loans), and you are able to earn a higher return on your investments. In that case, it may make sense to invest your money instead of paying off the debt. Additionally, suppose you have an emergency fund in place and are confident that you can continue to make your debt payments while investing. In that case, you may choose to invest your money.
Ultimately, the decision to pay off debt or invest should be based on your individual financial situation and goals. Therefore, it is important to consider factors such as your interest rates, potential investment returns, and overall financial stability before deciding. You can consult with a financial advisor who can provide personalized advice may be helpful.

Step 8: Invest in a retirement account.

Retirement planning is something that every person should prioritize, regardless of age or income level. Investing in a retirement account is one of the best ways to prepare for your golden years. There are several types of accounts to choose from, offered by your employer.

Investing in an account for retirement allows your money to grow tax-free, meaning you will only pay taxes on the money you earn once you withdraw it later in life.

Furthermore, many employers offer matching contributions for retirement accounts, which means free money. For example, if your employer offers a 50% match up to 6% of your salary, and you contribute 6% of your salary to account use for retirement, your employer will contribute an additional 3%.

In short, investing in an account for retirement is a good move that can help you build a nest egg for your future. It's never too early or too late to start, so take the first step toward a secure retirement and start investing today.

How much should I invest in a retirement account?

Investing in a retirement account is an important financial decision that requires careful consideration. The amount you should invest in an account for retirement depends on many factors and personal circumstances, such as your age, income, retirement goals, and current financial situation.

One common rule of thumb is to save at least 10-15% of your income for retirement. However, the actual amount you need to save depends on your individual circumstances. For example, if you start saving for retirement at a younger age, you can save less each year and still achieve your retirement goals.

A factor to consider is the type of retirement account you are investing in. For example, if you are investing in a traditional account for retirement, your contributions may be tax-deductible. This may reduce your current tax burden. On the other hand, if you are investing in certain retirement saving accounts, your contributions are made with after-tax dollars, but your withdrawals in retirement are tax-free.

The earlier you begin saving into a retirement account, the longer your funds will have to grow as a result of compound interest. Starting early can therefore have a significant impact in the long run, even if you can only afford to contribute a tiny sum each month.

Ultimately, the amount you should invest in a retirement account depends on your individual financial situation and goals. Therefore, consulting with a financial advisor or planner is important to determine the best investment strategy for your needs.

What should I invest my retirement account in?

Investing in an account for retirement can be a daunting task. Still, it is a critical step toward securing your financial future. The right investment strategy depends on your age, risk tolerance, and financial goals. However, some general guidelines can help you make an informed decision.

1. Diversify your portfolio: Diversification is essential to minimize risk and maximize returns. The exact allocation depends on your risk tolerance and investment horizon. For example, if you have a long investment horizon, you can afford to take more risks and invest in stocks. If you have a short investment horizon, you may want to invest in bonds and cash equivalents.
2. Consider index funds.
3. Be mindful of fees: Fees can eat into your returns over time. Make sure to invest in low-cost funds with minimal fees. A difference of 1% in fees can significantly impact your portfolio's growth over time.
4. Rebalance your portfolio regularly: Due to market fluctuations, your asset allocation may change over time.
5. Consult a financial advisor: If you need more clarification on your investment strategy, consider consulting a financial advisor. An advisor can help you assess your risk tolerance, set financial goals, and design a personalized investment plan.

Investing in an account for retirement requires careful consideration of your financial goals, risk tolerance, and investment horizon. You may make wise investment choices and safeguard your financial future by diversifying your portfolio, taking index funds into consideration, paying attention to fees, conducting regular portfolio rebalancing, and speaking with a financial advisor.

Step 9: Create a debt repayment plan.

A debt repayment plan is a strategy to pay off your debts organizationally and efficiently. It typically involves listing out all of your debts, prioritizing them based on interest rates or balances, and then creating a budget to allocate funds toward paying off those debts. A debt repayment plan aims to reduce the amount of interest you pay over time while also making progress toward becoming debt-free.

Creating a debt repayment plan can be overwhelming. Still, taking control of your finances and getting out of debt is important.

Steps to help you create a debt repayment plan:

1. List all your debts: Start by listing all your debts, including the creditor, interest rate, minimum payment, and balance owed.
2. Prioritize your debts: Next, prioritize your debts based on the interest rate or balance owed. You can choose to pay off the debt with the highest interest rate first, also known as the avalanche method, or pay off the smallest balance first, known as the snowball method.
3. Figure out how much money you can allocate towards monthly debt repayment.
4. Negotiate with creditors: Consider negotiating with your creditors to reduce interest rates or work out a payment plan that fits within your budget.
5. Stick to a plan: Once you have a debt repayment plan, it's important to stick to it.

Remember, creating a debt repayment plan takes time and discipline. However, the end result will be worth it as you work towards becoming debt-free.

Step 10: Automate your savings.

Are you tired of struggling to save money each month? Automating your savings may be the solution you've been looking for. You can save by setting up Pre-Autorised-Saving from your checking account to a savings or investment account.

First, determine how much you want to save each month. Ideally, this should be a percentage of your income, such as 1-5-10-20%. Then, set up automatic transfers on your bank's website or app. You can choose to transfer the money weekly, bi-weekly, or monthly depending on your pay schedule.

Automating your savings removes the hassle of saving money and can help you reach your financial goals faster.

Why should you automate your savings?

1. Automating your savings is one of the most thoughtful financial decisions you can make. Setting up Pre Autorised-Savings transfers from your checking account to your savings account can ensure that you are consistently putting money aside for your future goals. Here are a few reasons why automating your savings is a great idea:
2. Consistency: When you automate your savings, you create a consistent habit of saving money. You don't have to worry about remembering to transfer money each month, as the process is done automatically. This consistency will help you reach your financial goals faster.
3. Discipline: Automating your savings also helps you to develop discipline when it comes to your finances. By setting up a specific amount to transfer each month, you commit yourself to save that money. This can help you to resist the temptation to spend money on unnecessary purchases.
4. Easy to track: Automating your savings also makes tracking your progress toward your financial goals easier. You can easily monitor your savings account to see how much money you have saved and how close you are to reach your target.
5. Saves time: Automating your savings is a time-saving strategy. Instead of spending time each month manually transferring money, you can set it up once and forget about it. Automatic saving frees up time to focus on other aspects of your financial planning.

In short, automating your savings is a smart financial move that can help you to develop discipline, save time, and reach your financial goals faster.

Conclusion:

Mastering your money takes time and effort, but it is worth it in the long run. By setting financial goals, creating a budget, managing debt, and investing wisely, you can achieve financial freedom and live a more comfortable life. Remember to track your progress and adjust your plan as needed. With dedication and discipline, you can master your money and achieve your financial goals.

Each person's finances are different, and they should seek independent financial advice from a professional. Therefore, the book information does not serve as financial advice. The information in this book should not be relied upon to be accurate and complete. The information in the book does not constitute legal or other professional advice. Consult a professional advisor for legal, financial, or other advice.

This page was left blank so that you could make notes.

11

This page was left blank so that you could make notes.

12

This page was left blank so that you could make notes.

13

This page was left blank so that you could make notes.

14

This page was left blank so that you could make notes.

This page was left blank so that you could make notes.

This page was left blank so that you could make notes.

17

This page was left blank so that you could make notes.

18

This page was left blank so that you could make notes.

This page was left blank so that you could make notes.

This page was left blank so that you could make notes.

21

This page was left blank so that you could make notes.

This page was left blank so that you could make notes.

This page was left blank so that you could make notes.

This page was left blank so that you could make notes.